Amazing Planet Earth

EXTREME WEATHER

TERRY JENNINGS

A+

Smart Apple Media

Smart Apple Media
P.O. Box 3263
Mankato, MN 56002

Printed in the United States of America

Library of Congress Cataloging-in-Publication Data

Jennings, Terry J.
  Extreme weather / by Terry Jennings.
     p. cm. -- (Amazing planet earth)
  Includes index.
  ISBN 978-1-59920-369-0 (hardcover)
  1. Weather--Juvenile literature. I. Title.
  QC981.3.J45 2009
  551.55--dc22

                                 2009003401

Created by Q2AMedia
Editor: Michael Downey
Art Director: Rahul Dhiman
Designer: Ranjan Singh
Picture Researcher: Shreya Sharma
Line Artist: Sibi N. Devasia
Coloring Artist: Mahender Kumar

All words in **bold** can be found in the glossary on pages 30–31.

Web site information is correct at time of going to press. However, the publishers cannot
accept liability for any information or links found on third-party Web sites.

Picture credits
t=top b=bottom c=center l=left r=right
Cover Image: Sean Martin/ iStockphoto.
Back Cover Image: Jim Brooks/ U.S. Navy

Insides: iStockphoto: Title Page, Celso Pupo/ Shutterstock: 4, Sampete/ Dreamstime: 5, Operational Significant Event in Imagery/
NOAA: 6, Debbie Larson/ NOAA: 7, Sergio Dorantes/Corbis: 9, Mike Theiss/Ultimate Chase/Corbis: 10,NOAA: 11, Rocco
Macri/123RF: 12, Danny Johnston/Associated Press: 13, Severe Storm Damage/ Associated Press: 14, Larry Atherton/Associated Press:
15, Vicnt/ iStockphoto: 17, Robert Spencer/Associated Press: 18, Jason Reed/ Reuters: 19, Christopher Morris/Corbis: 20, Christopher
Morris/ Corbis: 21, Armando Franca/Associated Press: 24, Li Xiaoguo/ Associated press: 25, Associated Press: 26, Ricardo Azoury/
Corbis: 27, Ben Heys/Shutterstock: 28, Kim Kulish/Corbis: 29, Shutterstock: 31.

Q2AMedia Art Bank: 8, 16, 22, 23.

9 8 7 6 5 4 3 2 1

Contents

World's Weather

Hot or cold, windy or still, dry or wet, **weather** can make our lives pleasant or put us in extreme danger! Weather plays a big part in what we eat and drink, the type of clothes we wear, and the design of our homes.

Wind and Rain

Earth's weather is powered by the Sun. **Winds** start blowing when the Sun's heat warms up Earth's surface. This causes hot air to rise and cooler air to rush in to take its place. Clouds form when water **evaporates** from the world's seas and oceans as **water vapor**. As these clouds cool down, their moisture falls as rain, **hail**, sleet, or snow.

• Sunny weather is perfect for sunbathing on a Brazilian beach.

Wild Weather

From time to time, severe weather strikes with deadly results. Long heat waves and **droughts**, sudden **hurricanes** and **tornadoes**, or freezing-cold **blizzards** and **ice storms** can bring large areas of a country to a complete standstill. Sometimes, weather conditions can be so severe that large buildings are reduced to rubble during an extremely violent **storm**.

● A heavy winter snowfall causes a massive traffic jam.

DATA FILE

- When we talk about climate, we mean the typical weather of a particular place, large or small, that occurs over a long period of time.

- Since prehistoric times, the climate all around the world has changed many times.

- There is enough water vapor in the **atmosphere** to flood the entire world to a depth of 8.2 feet (2.5 m) if the water vapor was turned into liquid water.

- Clouds are made up of water droplets and **ice** crystals that are so tiny they can float in the air.

- The scientific name for rain is **precipitation**. This term also includes drizzle, snow, sleet, and hail.

Hurricane Mitch

Hurricanes are huge, powerful windstorms that can be hundreds of miles wide. They form in warm and wet conditions, usually over an ocean near Earth's equator.

Deadly Hurricane

Hurricane Mitch struck Central America in late 1998. It was the most deadly hurricane in this part of the world for more than 100 years. Moving in from the Atlantic Ocean, Mitch brought violent winds of up to 180 miles (290 km) per hour. A huge amount of rain caused devastating floods and **mud slides** in Honduras and Nicaragua. Mitch also caused ocean waves more than 20 feet (6 m) high. The floodwaters reached the third floors of some buildings in Honduras.

Name: Hurricane Mitch
Location: Central America
Date: Oct.–Nov. 1998
Weather type: Hurricane
Fatalities: More than 11,000
Path of hurricane: Shown by the arrows on the map

• A satellite photograph of Hurricane Mitch shows its swirling clouds around the calm center of the storm.

News Flash

November 1998

As Hurricane Mitch tore across Central America, the most deadly Atlantic storm in two centuries left a trail of destruction in its wake. About 11,000 people are believed to have been killed. Nicaragua and Honduras received the brunt of the storm. Development in some of the western hemisphere's poorest countries has been set back by as much as 50 years.

• Hurricane Mitch caused severe flooding. Parts of the capital of Honduras were buried under 40 feet (12 m) of mud and water.

Human Casualties

More than 3 million people were affected by the hurricane. Many hundreds of thousands of people faced disease and poverty as their homes and workplaces were destroyed. Roads collapsed, crops were ruined, and bridges and power lines were swept away. More than 11,000 people died as a result of the flooding and landslides and another 18,000 were missing. The damage was estimated at more than $5 billion. Many months after the hurricane, the people of Central America still struggled to rebuild their lives.

Life of a Hurricane

A hurricane takes several days to form and is one of the most powerful of all weather systems. During a storm, the destructive winds spiral around a central, low-pressure area called an **eye**.

Strong Winds

Hurricanes usually form over an ocean or a sea when the **temperature** of the air is higher than the temperature of the water. When this happens, water evaporates into the air and rises up, pulling in cooler air underneath. This movement of air leads to very strong winds that start to spin around the center, or eye, of the hurricane. North of the equator, the winds rotate in a counterclockwise direction. South of the equator, they turn clockwise.

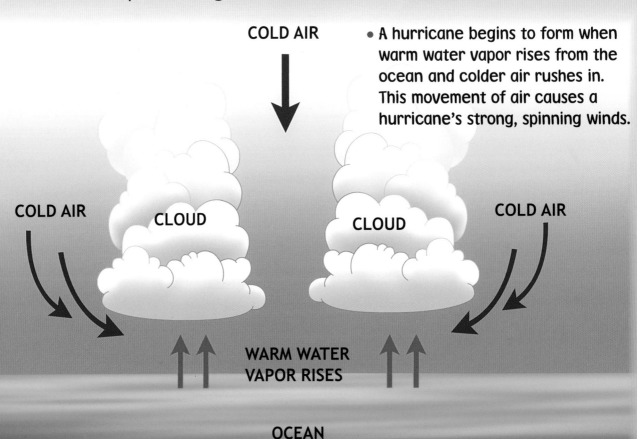

COLD AIR

COLD AIR

CLOUD

CLOUD

COLD AIR

WARM WATER VAPOR RISES

OCEAN

• A hurricane begins to form when warm water vapor rises from the ocean and colder air rushes in. This movement of air causes a hurricane's strong, spinning winds.

- In 1988, Hurricane Gilbert caused gigantic waves that lifted this boat from the ocean and dropped it on land.

Hitting Land

Some hurricanes die out before they reach land. Others get stronger and pick up more water as they move over a warm ocean. When a hurricane hits land, swirling winds can destroy buildings and huge waves pushed toward the shore can cause flooding. This movement of water is called a storm **surge**. Once the hurricane is far away from the warm ocean, its destructive power soon dies away.

DATA FILE

- A hurricane has wind speeds of 75 miles (120 km) per hour or more.

- Hurricanes are given names to help identify them. The names come from lists made by the World Meteorological Organization.

- On average, most hurricanes last between three to fourteen days.

- **Global warming** may cause many more hurricanes in the future.

- North of the equator, the hurricane season usually lasts about four months—from July to October.

- South of the equator, most hurricanes occur between November and March.

Hurricane Katrina

When a powerful, swirling hurricane makes its way onto dry land from the ocean, it almost always causes a massive amount of damage. This is especially the case when the hurricane leaves large areas flooded.

Name: Hurricane Katrina
Location: Southern U.S.
Date: August 2005
Weather type: Hurricane
Fatalities: More than 1,800
Path of hurricane: Shown by the arrows on the map

Developing Storm

On August 23, 2005, an area of low **air pressure**, called a **depression**, developed above the Atlantic Ocean north of Cuba. This depression was named Katrina when it turned into a storm. When Katrina reached Florida's coast two days later, its winds had reached destructive speeds of up to 80 miles (128 km) per hour.

• Hurricane Katrina's violent, spinning winds roared through the streets of New Orleans.

City Flooded

After Hurricane Katrina had crossed over the warm waters of the Florida Everglades, it passed into the Gulf of Mexico. The water temperature was a very warm 90°F (32°C). This warmth increased the speed of the spinning winds in the hurricane, which gave even more deadly power to the storm. Hurricane Katrina hit land in Louisiana. The huge storm surges caused vast amounts of water to break through the high banks, or levees, that protected the city of New Orleans. This led to sudden and severe flooding that killed many people in the city.

- Thousands of homes were flooded in New Orleans when the levees gave way.

DATA FILE

- A cyclone is a hurricane that forms over the Indian Ocean.

- Typhoon is the name for a hurricane that forms in the Pacific Ocean near the East Asian countries of Japan, China, and the Philippines.

- The most deadly cyclone struck Bangladesh in 1970. It killed at least 300,000 people.

- When typhoon Saomai hit southern China in 2006, about 300 people were killed and 1,000 ships were sunk.

Terrible Tornadoes

A tornado, sometimes called a twister, is a ferocious whirlwind. Tornadoes usually do not occur in winter, but there are exceptions. In February 2008, a series of deadly tornadoes struck the southern United States.

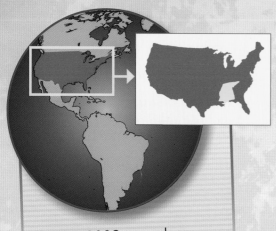

Name: 2008 tornadoes
Location: Southern U.S.
Date: February 2008
Weather type: Series of about 82 tornadoes
Fatalities: 59
Location of tornadoes: Shown by the yellow area on the map

A Series of Tornadoes

In February 2008, huge thunderstorms lashed southern parts of the United States. These were triggered when warm, moist air that was moving north met a band of very cold air. These thunderstorms produced about 82 tornadoes that affected a huge area. Many of these twisters brought destruction to densely populated areas in a number of states.

- In 2008, tornadoes ripped their way through the southern United States, causing massive destruction.

Warning Sirens

People awoke during the night to the sound of shattering glass and warning sirens. Horrified, those that could ran for safety as tornadoes flung trailer homes into the air, flattened trees and factories, and destroyed thousands of houses. In Macon County, Tennessee, a 74-year-old man, whose trailer home had been destroyed, was killed by another tornado as he waited for an ambulance to take him to the hospital.

News Flash
February 2008

Dozens of tornadoes sliced across the southern United States. They ripped apart homes and shopping malls. At least 59 people were killed and hundreds more were injured. Officials reported 28 people were killed in Tennessee, 13 in Arkansas, and 7 in Kentucky.

- A woman searches for personal items in the ruins of her house after tornadoes struck parts of Alabama.

Disaster in Tennessee

In Tennessee, 28 people died. A shopping mall
collapsed, and an explosion at a natural gas plant
shot flames more than 490 feet (150 m) into the
air. A police radio tower was destroyed. This made
it extremely difficult for emergency services to
communicate with each other in order to rescue
people who were trapped under rubble.

Students Injured

At Union University, in Jackson, Mississippi, two
living areas were destroyed and many students were
injured. One student, who was playing pinball at the
time, was pulled out of a building by the wind. Winds
hurled him through the air while he was still holding
onto the pinball machine.

Rescue Work

In Shelby County, Tennessee, three people were killed when they ran for shelter to a nearby warehouse and the roof fell in on them. In many states, National Guard troops were called out to assist. Rescuers moved from house to house looking for trapped residents. Many people, some clinging to lengths of wood to stay afloat, were pulled out from swollen rivers. Fallen power lines and blocked roads hampered much of the rescue work.

● Vehicles and buildings were wrecked by the destructive whirlwinds.

DATA FILE

- The 2008 U.S. tornadoes traveled close to the ground for long distances of up to 50 miles (80 km). These twisters are known as long track tornadoes.

- Tornadoes do not normally occur in winter. The unusually warm weather that triggered the 2008 tornadoes may have been caused by global warming.

- Some of the hailstones were 4 inches (11 cm) in diameter.

- The deadliest U.S. tornadoes occurred in March 1925. These left 695 people dead and more than 2,000 injured.

How Tornadoes Form

Tornadoes usually form from thunderclouds and appear suddenly. Little or no warning can be given to the unfortunate people in their path.

Tight Funnel

Tornadoes often appear in groups, usually far inland, away from the ocean. They normally form during violent thunderstorms, when a hot, fast-moving, upward air current meets a cold downward air current. The hot and cold currents spiral around each other and form a tight funnel between a **cumulonimbus** thundercloud and the ground. This rotating column of air quickly moves across the land, smashing objects in its path.

- Tornadoes are extremely violent, rotating columns of air that reach down from a cumulonimbus thundercloud to the ground.

CUMULONIMBUS CLOUD

LIGHTNING

HOT AIR RISING

Trail of Destruction

Smaller and much faster than a hurricane, a tornado can leave a trail of destruction 1.2 miles (2 km) wide and 50 miles (80 km) long on the ground. Tornadoes have internal wind speeds of up to 300 miles (480 km) per hour and can flatten large buildings, uproot trees, and hurl vehicles. Tornadoes can strike very quickly, but good planning can increase the chances of survival. Basements in buildings and houses have saved many lives.

- **Waterspouts** are similar to tornadoes but form over water and are usually much weaker.

DATA FILE

- Tornadoes develop beneath huge thunderclouds that are produced along cold **fronts**.

- The United States has the most violent tornadoes. There are about 1,000 every year.

- A violent tornado killed 160 people and injured 2,000 when it tracked through coastal villages in India in March 1998.

- In 1963, a tornado in northwest Assam, India, killed 139 people and left 3,760 families homeless in 33 villages.

- England has the most tornadoes per square kilometer (.39 square mile), but they are quite weak, so usually no one notices them.

Freezing Blizzard

Blizzards cause serious problems and can put people in danger. Heavy snowfall and high winds bring down power lines, leaving communities without electricity. Travel may also be impossible during severe blizzards.

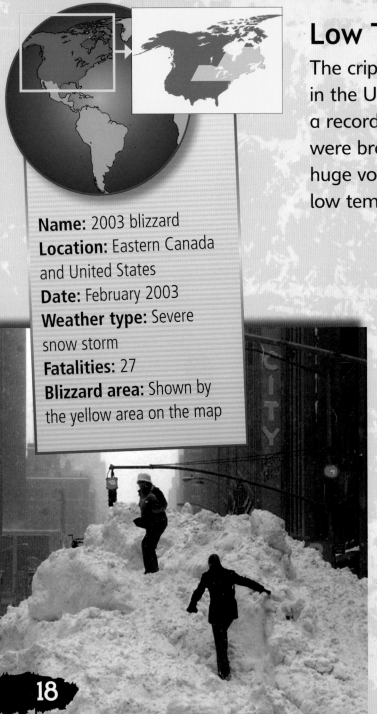

Name: 2003 blizzard
Location: Eastern Canada and United States
Date: February 2003
Weather type: Severe snow storm
Fatalities: 27
Blizzard area: Shown by the yellow area on the map

Low Temperatures

The crippling February 2003 blizzard in the United States and Canada was a record-breaking event. Major cities were brought to a standstill due to the huge volume of snow and record low temperatures.

Ice and Snow

The storm started in southern parts of the United States with a heavy torrential rain. As the storm moved north, temperatures dropped and water quickly turned to ice on the ground. Massive amounts of snow started falling. Some cities reported layers of snow up to 3.3 feet (1 m) high. At times, more than 4 inches (10 cm) of snow fell in an hour.

● Snow piled up on the streets of New York City enabled people to have a close-up view of traffic lights.

18

Schools Closed

As the blizzard worsened, airports closed and road travel was impossible. People could not move about, and rescue services were hampered in their attempts to keep towns and cities functioning. In Baltimore, Maryland, the roof of a railroad museum collapsed under the weight of snow and damaged many valuable engines. Most schools closed for at least a week. With so much snow on the roads and nowhere to put it, some snowplows were forced to push the snow into school parking lots and playgrounds, causing more schools to close.

News Flash
February 2003

In New York City, heavy snow and ice have made conditions very difficult. Airports have been closed, trains canceled, and streets made impassable to cars. Many sidewalks have been blocked by snow, so people walked down the city's wide, plowed streets to get from place to place.

• During the freezing conditions, anti-icing liquid was sprayed on runways so aircraft could land and take off.

Deadly Ice Storm

When rain freezes as soon as it touches the ground, scientists call the result an ice storm. In January 1998, one of the worst ice storms hit Canada.

Name: Canadian ice storm
Location: Canada and northeast United States
Date: January 1998
Weather type: Freezing rain, ice pellets, and snow
Fatalities: 28
Ice storm area: Shown by the yellow areas on the map

Freezing Rain

For six days in January 1998, three storms of freezing rain and snow coated many parts of Ontario, Quebec, and New Brunswick in Canada with up to 4.3 inches (11 cm) of ice. The freezing rain started on January 5, 1998, just as many Canadians were returning to work after the Christmas holidays. It continued to fall for more than 80 hours. Usually, freezing rain lasts for only a few hours.

● **The weight of ice caused tree branches to snap and fall during the ice storms.**

Power Failure

Heavy ice brought down power and telephone lines, forcing 600,000 people to seek shelter in hotels and hastily built shelters. Temperatures kept on falling, in places plunging below -40°F (-40°C). More than 4 million people lost their electricity. Freezing winds blowing from the Arctic chilled the air further, killing thousands of cows. Millions of trees fell, and many more died during the rest of the winter.

DATA FILE

- During the 1998 Canadian ice storm, 28 people died—many from **hypothermia**, and 945 people were seriously injured.

- More than 130 massive electricity towers were destroyed and about 30,000 electricity and telephone poles fell during the storm.

- Around 16,000 Canadian troops were brought in to help clean up.

- Farmers dumped about 2.6 million gallons (10 million L) of milk as milk-processing plants were shut.

- Most of the sugar maple tree plantations, which are used by Quebec's maple syrup producers, were permanently destroyed.

- This was the most expensive natural disaster in Canada's history. The cost of the storms was estimated at U.S. $3.5 billion (Can $5 billion).

- Canadian Army soldiers work to repair power lines brought down during the ice storms that left many homes without heat or light.

Blizzards and Ice Storms

A covering of snow on the ground or a coating of ice crystals on trees can look attractive. However, there are times when heavy snow and ice can be deadly.

Snow Formation

When water vapor freezes around dust particles in the atmosphere, tiny ice crystals are produced. These crystals gradually join together to form snowflakes, which fall to the ground when they are heavy enough. When thick snow, low temperatures, and strong winds all happen at the same time, blizzards can occur. A phenomenon known as a whiteout sometimes accompanies a blizzard. This is when heavy snow and low clouds make it impossible to tell where the ground ends and the sky begins.

• Snow formation

WATER VAPOR FREEEZES INTO ICE CRYSTALS

ICE CRYSTALS JOIN TO MAKE SNOWFLAKES

• Blizzard formation

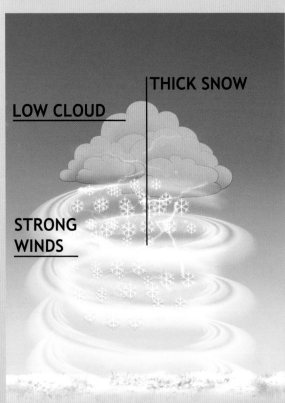

THICK SNOW

LOW CLOUD

STRONG WINDS

Supercooled Droplets

In wintry conditions, when temperatures at cloud level are below the freezing point, water droplets that fall from clouds will be **supercooled**. They are likely to freeze as soon as they meet a colder layer below the freezing point. When large, supercooled droplets fall on ground that is below the freezing point, they spread out and freeze. This quickly covers surfaces with a layer of ice that makes walking or driving difficult. The weight of this ice on overhead wires and tree branches may bring them crashing down.

CLOUDS BELOW FREEZING POINTS

• Ice storm formation

SUPERCOOLED LARGE DROPLETS

FROZEN GROUND

Raging Heat Wave

Record high temperatures and a severe lack of rain were responsible for the deaths of some 35,000 people in Europe in the summer of 2003. Many of the victims were the very young and the elderly.

Raging Fires

The summer of 2003 was probably the hottest in Europe in 500 years. Temperatures reached 104°F (40°C) for more than 20 days. The temperatures recorded in the United Kingdom were the highest ever. Weeks of heat and lack of rain had a devastating effect on farm crops throughout Europe, and thousands of cattle, pigs, and chickens died. Fires raged in many European countries. In Portugal, 531,000 acres (215,000 ha) of forests were destroyed by fire. Glaciers began to melt in Switzerland, railway lines buckled, and road surfaces melted.

• An aircraft drops water onto a **wildfire** to try to put out the flames during the European heat wave of 2003.

Water Shortages

The heat in 2003 caused severe water shortages and health problems. Rivers and **reservoirs** used for domestic water supply or to produce hydro-electric power either dried up or became dangerously low. In Serbia, the Danube River fell to its lowest level in 100 years, revealing bombs and tanks from World War II. In France, which relies on nuclear power for more than 75 percent of its electricity, many nuclear power stations had to shut down. The river water they needed to cool their reactors had become too warm and the water levels too low.

- In 2003, a severe lack of water also affected China. Here, a farmer examines his corn crop, which was destroyed by drought.

Severe Drought

In 2005, a severe drought in South America's Amazon Basin left parts of the region extremely dry. Trees and crops withered, fires raged, fish died, and deadly diseases spread to many parts of the region.

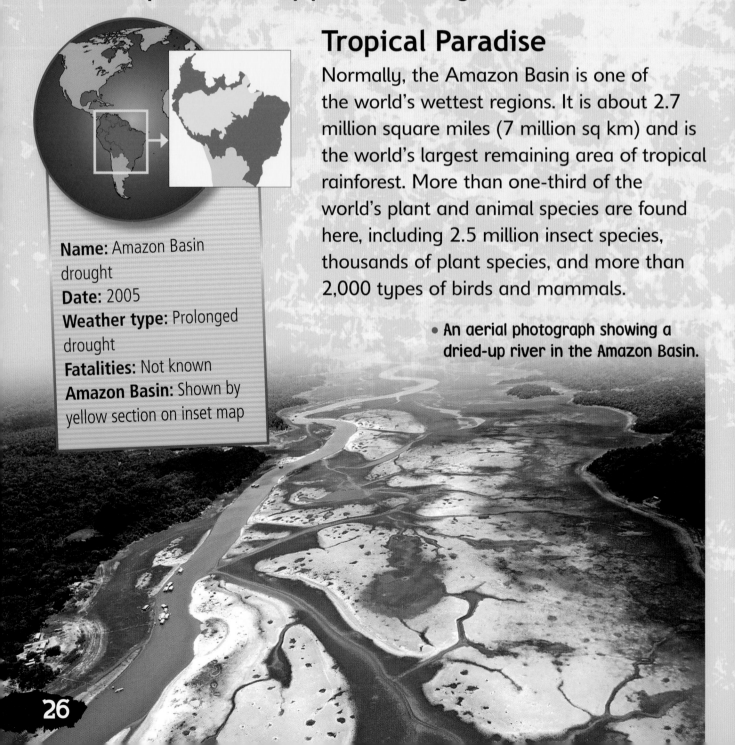

Name: Amazon Basin drought
Date: 2005
Weather type: Prolonged drought
Fatalities: Not known
Amazon Basin: Shown by yellow section on inset map

Tropical Paradise

Normally, the Amazon Basin is one of the world's wettest regions. It is about 2.7 million square miles (7 million sq km) and is the world's largest remaining area of tropical rainforest. More than one-third of the world's plant and animal species are found here, including 2.5 million insect species, thousands of plant species, and more than 2,000 types of birds and mammals.

• **An aerial photograph showing a dried-up river in the Amazon Basin.**

• During the drought of 2005, drinking water had to be taken by truck to towns and villages in the Amazon Basin.

Worst Drought

In 2005, the most severe drought on record blighted the Amazon Basin. Thousands of fish died, and villages were cut off as waterways dried up. People walked or rode bicycles in places normally used by canoes and riverboats. Boats became stuck in mud. Forest fires raged as trees and other plants dried out. There was a severe shortage of clean water to drink, and fish were no longer available to eat. Stagnant, muddy pools allowed malaria-carrying mosquitoes to breed rapidly. Even worse, the lack of water meant that raw sewage was not removed. This allowed deadly diseases, such as cholera, to spread rapidly.

DATA FILE

- The Amazon River drains a vast region that is very nearly the size of Australia.

- Experts think that deforestation, or the clearing of large areas of forest, made the drought worse.

- The drought in South America's Amazon Basin was accompanied by a record hurricane season in North America.

- In the Brazilian city of Manaus, the level of the Amazon dropped 10 feet (3 m) lower than average.

Power of the Sun

Droughts occur when there is little or no rain over a long period of time. Almost one-third of Earth's land suffers from droughts that affect more than 600 million people.

Cloudless Skies

A heat wave is a period of very hot weather. In summer, if there are few or no clouds, the air and the ground are heated up by the Sun. The longer the sky remains cloudless, the longer the heat wave will last. People who do not protect themselves during a heat wave can become quite ill. Their hands, feet, and ankles can swell up, and they may get headaches and feel sick.

● Reservoirs can dry up during a heat wave.

Using Water Wisely

Many countries around the world suffer from heat waves and drought. This is a problem that is likely to worsen in the future. Very hot temperatures can make droughts even worse. Sometimes, droughts can last for years. When this happens, the land dries up and becomes so hard that plants find it difficult to grow, even when it starts raining again. If we learn to use water wisely and not waste it, some of the problems that are caused by heat waves and drought can be avoided.

DATA FILE

- **Deserts** suffer from permanent drought. Many tropical areas have a seasonal drought, which is called the dry season.

- The area of land affected by serious drought has more than doubled since the 1970s. It now affects about 30 percent of the world's land surface.

- Drought has brought many famines to African countries, such as the Sudan and Ethiopia.

• A raging wildfire sweeps toward beach homes and businesses during a drought in Malibu, California, in 1992.

Glossary

air pressure the weight of Earth's atmosphere pressing down on its surface

atmosphere the thick layer of air that surrounds Earth

blizzard a very heavy snowfall accompanied by strong winds

cumulonimbus a large, billowing, flat-topped cloud that is often called a thundercloud

depression an area of the atmosphere where the air pressure is lower than that of surrounding areas

desert a dry region with very few plants

drought an unusually long period of dry weather

equator the imaginary line around the center of Earth

evaporate when water is heated, it changes from a liquid to a gas and disappears as water vapor

eye a fairly calm, clear area at the center of a hurricane

front the forward edge of a mass of warm or cold air

global warming a general warming of Earth's climate brought about by an increase of polluting gases, such as carbon dioxide, that reduce the amount of the Sun's heat that escapes into space

hail a type of precipitation that falls as pellets of ice

hurricane a swirling storm found in tropical parts of the Atlantic Ocean—they are called cyclones or typhoons in Asia

hypothermia the gradual lowering of body temperature due to heat loss in cold weather that causes a person to become drowsy, fall unconscious, or die if untreated

ice the solid form of water when it freezes

ice storm a heavy rainstorm in which the rain freezes as soon as it touches the ground or some other solid object, the temperature of which is below freezing point

mud slide the movement of a mass of mud down the side of a hill or mountain

precipitation water falling from the clouds as rain, drizzle, hail, sleet, or snow

reservoir a large, artificial lake used to store drinking water, produce electricity, or prevent a river from flooding

storm a period of violent weather that usually has strong winds, dark clouds, and heavy rain, hail, or snow

supercooled water that is cooled below its freezing point but does not turn to ice

surge a sudden rush of water

temperature the measure of how hot or cold something is

tornado a violent, whirling column of air that appears as a dark cloud shaped like a funnel, also called a twister

tropics the regions near the equator that have a hot climate all year round and lie between the Tropic of Cancer in the north and the Tropic of Capricorn in the south

waterspout a tornado over the ocean or sea

water vapor the gas or mist that forms when water is heated

weather how hot or cold, wet or dry, still or moving the air is at a particular time

whirlwind a strong wind that whirls around or blows in a spiral

wildfire a fire that burns grassland, forest, scrub, bush, or other wild plant life

wind air moving from place to place

Index

Web Sites

http://www.drought.unl.edu/kids/
This kid-friendly site explains what a drought is and its impact. Photos and maps are provided.

http://www.nationalgeographic.com/ngkids/0308/hurricane/path.html
Kids can learn about hurricanes, typhoons, and cyclones.

http://www.weatherwizkids.com/winter_storms.htm
This site offers kids information on blizzards and how they form. It also discusses snowflakes, wind chill, and frostbite.